Prologue – The Moment Time Stood ⸹

There are moments in life that split everything into a *before* and an *after*. For me, it was a Monday. Ordinary in every way—until it wasn't. I can still hear the doctor's voice, calm but heavy, delivering the words that shattered our world: *"There's a 4cm tumor on your daughter's brain."*

In that instant, time stopped. The sterile walls of the hospital seemed to close in. and my breath caught somewhere between disbelief and desperation. I remember looking at her—my daughter, full of life and laughter, her eyes wide with confusion but somehow still calm. She didn't understand yet. How could she? I barely did.

Then I looked at her dad. The fear in his eyes mirrored mine. No words passed between us—just a shared, paralyzing disbelief. In that moment, everything we thought we knew about our lives, our future, and our daughter collapsed into something unrecognizable. We were parents, yes—but now we were soldiers standing at the edge of a battlefield we didn't know how to cross.

From that moment on, we were thrust into a world we never asked to enter—of MRIs and medications, neurosurgeons and night sweats, hope and helplessness. It was a battle we didn't choose, but one we would fight every single day.

This book is our story—told through my eyes, with glimpses into hers. It's a record of pain and perseverance, of fear and fierce love. It's not just about the diagnosis or the treatments. It's about what it means to watch your child endure something unimaginable, and how, in the darkest moments, her strength taught me how to be strong.

If you are reading this because you're walking a similar path, I want you to know: you are not alone. This journey may break you—but it can also build you in ways you never expected. This is for the parents holding their breath in waiting rooms, the siblings trying to be brave, the children who never stop fighting, and the families who somehow carry on. This is our truth.

This is *Through Her Eyes*.
Chapter One – Before the Storm

Before the MRI.

Before the sterile words and the hospital lights.

Before we were told there was a 4cm tumor on her brain—there was the girl I knew and raised and fought beside for years.

She was 21 when we heard the words that changed

everything. But her fight had started long before that day.

Since she was 13, she'd been battling demons no one could see. Diagnoses came slowly, painfully—borderline personality disorder, complex PTSD, anxiety, depression. There were moments of deep darkness, but also fierce defiance. She was brilliant, misunderstood, layered. Suspected autism added to the complexity of how she saw the world—and how the world often failed to see her back.

She lived in sharp contrast: vulnerable and bold, tired but tenacious. Her mind was loud and fast-moving, her heart big enough to carry others even when her own pain felt unbearable. We learned early how to navigate mental health services, medication side effects, crisis lines, the long silences and the desperate cries. So when the physical symptoms began, we were already worn—but still standing. It started with the double vision. She

mentioned it casually at first, almost like it was funny.

"Everything has a twin," she said one day. Then came the

headaches. Not just annoying ones—deep,

behind-the-eyes pain that made her nauseous. She began

vomiting without warning. Then one day I noticed her

eyes. Her pupils didn't react to light. And one eye began

to drift outward, like a lazy squint. I told myself not to

panic. She had been through so much—surely this was

just another complication. We were used to doctors not

having answers.

We went to the optician first. They updated

her prescription. Told us to monitor it. But the

symptoms didn't improve. They got worse.

So we went to the GP. I explained everything—twice.

The GP examined her briefly, said it was likely a visual

alignment issue and recommended a prism to correct the squint. Another trip back to the optician. This time, they weren't convinced. Something about her pupils, the lack of reaction—they weren't happy.

They didn't say it out loud, but I saw it in their eyes. Concern. Urgency.

They contacted the GP themselves. I still remember the quiet alarm in their tone. Not panicked—but firm. The GP responded, and finally, we were booked for an urgent MRI. It was set for May 24, 2021.

I didn't know it then, but that would become the line in our lives—the moment where everything we thought we understood about her body, her mind, and our future would shift into something we never saw coming. That Monday morning, I hoped for answers. What we got was devastation.

Chapter Two – The Diagnosis

May 24, 2021.

That date is etched into me forever. The day our world cracked open.

We thought we were just going in for an MRI. A precaution. Another test in a long string of appointments. Lizzie was quiet that morning, tired, worn down by weeks of headaches, vomiting, and double vision. Her eyes—her beautiful, expressive eyes—no longer reacted to light. One had started drifting outward, giving her a faraway look that unsettled me more than I wanted to admit.

The MRI felt endless. I sat in that cold waiting room, forcing myself not to spiral. I told myself it would be fine. It *had* to be fine.

But then we were called into a small room.

A doctor sat across from us, serious but kind. And then

he said it—those words I will never forget:

"There's a 4cm tumor on your daughter's brain."

I broke.

I cried out—*"No, no, no!"*—like if I said it enough times,

it wouldn't be true. The tears came hard, the kind that

steal your breath and shake your whole body. But even in

that moment—*her* moment—Lizzie reached for *me*. She

grabbed my hand, looked me in the eye, and said, *"It's*

okay, I've got you."

Like *I* was the one who was sick.

Like *she* needed to take care of *me*.
And in that moment, I didn't know whether to feel pride
or heartbreak.

When the doctor left, I couldn't breathe. I told her dad I

needed some air, and he stayed with her while I walked outside. I didn't know who to call, what to do. My body was in fight-or-flight, my mind spinning.

For some reason, I rang my boss.

I was off sick at the time, dealing with a flare-up of my fibromyalgia. I don't even remember what I was thinking—I just needed someone to know. As soon as she picked up, the words flew out of my mouth like a scream:

"She has a brain tumor."

And then I crumbled.

I sobbed into the phone, hyperventilating, barely able to speak. I could hear the shock and compassion in her voice, but I couldn't make sense of her response. I just needed to say it out loud. To make it real. To stop it from swallowing me whole.

When I returned to the ward, the hospital told us they were going to keep Lizzie in overnight for more tests. In the morning, she'd be transferred to the larger general hospital for urgent neurology care. And then came the part that nearly broke us again—we had to leave. We had to leave our daughter, our girl, alone in that hospital room, with machines beeping softly and fear hanging in the air like fog. And we had to drive home, faces wet with tears, hearts shredded, and sit down with her siblings to tell them the unthinkable: That their sister had a brain tumor.

And everything had changed.

Chapter Three – The Transfer

That night felt like a blur.

After leaving Lizzie at the hospital, we got in the car and began the heartbreaking task of telling our family. We drove from one place to the next—my parents, who are divorced. Jason's mum and stepdad. His dad had passed away in 2012—from brain cancer, of all things. That added a layer of fear that neither of us said out loud, but we both felt. We told my sisters, Jason's sisters, our brothers. And then there was Jason's eldest daughter—my stepdaughter—who took it like a punch to the heart.

We must've looked like ghosts showing up at each door, reliving the moment over and over: *"It's a brain tumor. 4cm. Pressing on her brain."* Watching faces crumble. Hearing the same shocked silences and the soft words of comfort we couldn't actually absorb.

By morning, we were back with Lizzie.

We were allowed to drive her to the general hospital ourselves. That was a small mercy—it meant we could go home first. She wanted to choose her own things. We packed a bag together: her favorite hoodie, some comfy joggers, her skincare bits, chargers, snacks. And before heading to the hospital, we took a detour—she wanted to see my mum. They've always been close, and even though we were all terrified, seeing each other helped settle some of that rising panic. It felt like we were doing something right in a world that suddenly made no sense.

When we got to the general hospital, everything was strict and sterile. Masks, testing—Covid rules still in place. We went through the process quietly, moving through corridors that felt too bright, too clean, too cold. Lizzie was placed on a ward first. Hours passed in a blur. Nurses came and went. Tests were done. Monitors beeped.

Then, while sitting there beside her, my phone rang.

It was the GP surgery.

They'd just received the results of the MRI from the day before and were calling to tell me that Lizzie had a brain tumor—and that she would be seen within two weeks. I stared at my phone in disbelief.

Two weeks?

They were calling *now*?

Over the *phone*?

Good job I already knew.

Good job we were already here.

I told them that, bluntly. That we were already in

hospital. Already admitted. Already with neurology.
Then I ended the call before I could say anything I'd
regret.

Eventually, a private room became available. I was
allowed to stay with her—another small gift. I helped
her settle in, made sure she had everything she needed,
and for a brief moment, it felt like we could breathe
again.

Jason had to leave. Covid rules meant only one of us
could stay, and he had to get back home to update the rest
of the family—especially Lizzie's siblings.

Her sister was 20 and trying to be strong. Her little
brother was just 13 at the time, on the autism spectrum
and attending a specialist school. We had to be careful in
how we told him, how we explained what was happening
without terrifying him. Another layer to this complex

nightmare.

That night, as the hospital quieted and Lizzie drifted in and out of sleep beside me, I sat in the chair next to her bed, trying to make sense of it all.

We were in the middle of it now. No turning back.

Just one day at a time.

One breath at a time.

Chapter Four – Diagnosis and Determination

We stayed in that hospital room for a week.

It became our strange little world—white walls, constant beeping, nurses coming and going in masks, and a window that let in just enough daylight to remind us the world outside still existed.

On the third day, Lizzie had her first brain surgery. She was in theatre for four hours. They performed a biopsy to determine the nature of the tumor and drilled a small hole into the front of her skull to relieve the pressure from the fluid buildup—hydrocephalus. The tumor had been blocking the normal flow of cerebrospinal fluid, causing it to pool in her brain. That explained her headaches, the sickness, the double vision, and why her eye had started to drift outward.

The tumor was located in the pineal region—a deep and delicate part of the brain, not easy to reach, and surrounded by critical structures. The biopsy would tell us what kind of tumor it was, but until then, we could only wait.

Because of Covid restrictions, Jason wasn't allowed in during that week. It was just Lizzie and me. We were both tested every other day, navigating our own kind of isolation in a hospital full of fear and uncertainty. Jason and I would meet outside the building, masked and distant, and I'd give him updates. He video called Lizzie every day, trying to bridge the distance with love and encouragement.

Lizzie struggled with the recovery. The release of pressure inside her skull sent her balance spinning. She had vertigo and constant nausea. For days, she was vomiting and unable to keep anything down. It was hard to see her so vulnerable, so tired—but still, she

didn't complain. She just kept going.

After a week of blood tests and slow improvement, we

were finally allowed to go home. We wouldn't have the

biopsy results for around three weeks. It felt like walking

out into the world with a ticking clock inside

us—knowing something was there but not yet knowing

what it really meant.

Then came the 16th of June.

That's the day we got the results. I shared them with

friends and family through Lizzie's Facebook

group—the place where we kept everyone updated,

where people poured in love and support when we

needed it most. This is what I wrote:

"Hi everyone,

So I know you've all been waiting for an update.

The consultant said it's in between benign and not. I'm not fully sure how that works but it's stage 2. He said she won't need chemo, as it doesn't work on this type of tumor anyway. She will be having it removed on 1st July, which is a very long operation and not without risk. However, it's the best option for her.

She may need radiotherapy after removal, but they will decide that later. This is going to be a long road to recovery and she will be in hospital for some months.

As usual, Lizzie has taken this in her stride and remained calm and composed throughout the consultation. He even said to her how amazing she is and how well she composed herself. He said he could see her determination and strength, and that now he's made a plan, he doesn't change his plans—so it will happen as he plans it, and she will be OK in his hands. Once again we thank you all for your love and support throughout this difficult time."

In those words, I tried to capture what we were all feeling: fear, hope, disbelief, and awe. Because Lizzie—my beautiful, brave girl—was taking all of this with grace I couldn't always match. Even the neurosurgeon saw it in her. Her calm, her strength, her quiet resolve. Now we had a date.

July 1st.

The day her life would change again.

The day we would put everything in the hands of a surgeon—and hope.

Chapter Five – Naming the Enemy

We finally had a name.

Stage 2 atypical meningioma.

A rare, stubborn tumor growing in a deep part of her brain—the pineal region. It wasn't fully benign, but it wasn't considered outright malignant either. It sat somewhere in the middle. Aggressive enough to need removing, but slow-growing enough to give us some hope.

Chemotherapy wouldn't work—not with this type of tumor. Radiotherapy might be needed after surgery, depending on how much they could remove and how it responded. But the next step was already decided: surgery. A long and risky procedure that would take hours.

It was a lot to process. The doctors were clear about the risks, but their confidence

gave us something to hold onto. So did Lizzie.

A couple of days after the consultation, while we were at

home, Lizzie came downstairs with a cheeky smirk on

her face.

"I've decided," she said, flopping onto the sofa. "If

I've got to have a brain tumor, I'm at least giving it a

name."

I raised my eyebrows, unsure what she was about to say.

She grinned. *"B-nard the B-stard."*

I laughed—really laughed. Through the tightness in my

chest, through the fear. It was such a Lizzie thing to do.

Somehow, in the face of everything, she found her

power. And she didn't stop there.

The next day, she actually wrote up an *eviction notice*—handwritten, in her boldest pen—and taped it to her bedroom wall.

"You're not living rent-free in my head anymore, B-nard," she declared. That was it. The battle had begun.

From that moment forward, we all referred to it that way. The doctors, the nurses, her friends, her siblings. "B-nard the B-stard" became the enemy. It gave us something to joke about, something to focus our anger and fear on. It was her way of taking back control—and in doing so, she gave the rest of us permission to breathe again.

We spent the days leading up to surgery getting

things ready. She packed her bag, double-checked her playlist, and even planned what hoodie to wear on the way to the hospital. She stayed focused, calm, determined.

Meanwhile, I was quietly managing the practicalities—making sure the house was in order, knowing Lizzie's 20-year-old sister would look after her 13-year-old brother while we were away. I didn't need to worry about time off work, as I was still signed off sick with fibromyalgia and would be for the next year. That gave me the space to focus entirely on Lizzie.

She had one goal:

Evict B-nard.

July 1st was circled on the calendar.

And none of us would ever forget it.

Chapter Six – The Eviction: Surgery Day

July 1st, 2021.

Eviction day.

We arrived at the hospital early, the sky low and grey with that strange, heavy stillness that comes with waiting for something life-changing. Lizzie sat in the back of the car, earbuds in, calm as ever. She wasn't scared—not visibly, anyway. Maybe she was hiding it for our sake. Maybe she was just that brave.

We made our way to the pre-op ward together. Once she was checked in, they told us that only one of us could stay with her from that point on. Covid rules again. Jason had to say goodbye right there.

He hugged her tightly, whispering something into her hair. I could see the heartbreak on his face as he walked away, and I knew

how much it tore him up to leave her like that. He waited

for me in the hospital cafeteria while I stayed by Lizzie's

side. We sat together in the sterile white of the pre-op

room, time dragging its feet. I held her hand, stroked her

hair, tried to be brave. She, as always, was composed.

When the call came and they began to wheel her away,

she turned to me and smiled.

"It's eviction day, Mum. Time to kick B-nard out."

I kissed her forehead, whispered that I loved her more
than anything, and then she was gone.

Jason and I didn't leave the hospital that day. I

couldn't. The thought of going home and waiting

there was unbearable. Instead, we sat in the

cafeteria, nursing endless

cups of coffee, wandering outside to the car

park for smoke breaks we didn't even

enjoy—just a way to breathe. (We've both

given up now, thankfully.)

Time passed in excruciating silence. We stared at the

same walls, checked our phones a hundred times, spoke

in low voices. No news. No idea how it was going. We

were simply… waiting.

Finally, at around **8:30pm**, we called the surgical ward. A

nurse told us to go home—they would call us with

updates, and we wouldn't be allowed to see Lizzie until

the next day anyway. I didn't want to leave, but I knew

we were no good to her exhausted and unraveling. So we

went.

At **9:30pm**, the surgeon called.

B-nard was out.

Lizzie was still in surgery—being closed up—but the main part was over. He told us he believed he'd removed the entire tumor, though an MRI would be done the next day to confirm. He sounded calm, confident, and incredibly kind. I remember clinging to his words like a lifeline.

The operation had taken **14 hours**.

Fourteen long, terrifying hours.

Lizzie was taken straight to ICU.

The next morning, I called for an update, heart pounding as the phone rang. Here's the post I shared that day on Lizzie's Facebook group:

Morning lovelies. A few of you have asked for an update... So I've spoken to the ward this morning. She's had a very good night. They've been slowly weaning down the sedation overnight. They are going to try removing the ventilator later today and wake her up properly. Some slight weakness on her left side but the surgeon said that's not unexpected and should go. Due to covid restrictions in ICU I can't be with her all day, but they have given me a 1-hour visiting slot at 4pm. I'll update again when I'm home. Thank you all for your love.

That visit at 4pm felt like waiting for Christmas and doomsday all at once.

But for now, the most important thing was this: Lizzie had survived.

B-nard had not.

Chapter Seven – Recovery Begins

Lizzie was in ICU for three days. They reduced the sedation slowly, and it took the full three days for her to properly wake up. Because of strict Covid restrictions, I was only allowed to visit her for one hour every other day. Jason wasn't allowed in at all.

I would sneak photos of her when the curtains were pulled—photos weren't allowed in ICU, but I needed to capture those moments, to remember that she was still here. I held her hand and talked to her, hoping she could hear me. From time to time, she would squeeze my hand—just enough to let me know she could.

At the end of day three, Lizzie was transferred to the neuro ward. She was awake now, but silent. She mouthed words but no sound came out. She couldn't move either—not even swallow. She had a feeding tube in and a catheter for the toilet. It was like her body had forgotten how to be.

This would mark the beginning of a long and difficult journey—learning everything again from scratch.

Lizzie would tell me later that she didn't even realize she wasn't speaking out loud. She thought we were ignoring her. My heart broke when she said that.

Her voice started to return about ten days later, in the most unexpected way. She got a nosebleed and suddenly started shouting, "NOSE BLEED! NOSE BLEED!" for the nurses. We laughed through tears—it was like the sound of hope.

On July 18th, Lizzie turned 22. Still in hospital. Thanks to the amazing community on her Facebook group, I brought in hundreds of cards and presents.

Because it was a Sunday and the clinic room next to the ward was closed, the staff allowed us to use it for a small celebration. It was just for an hour, but it meant the world.

Jason, Ellie, Kian, my mum and I were all there. Lizzie's voice was still quiet and slurred. She had limited movement in her arms and hands, and none in her legs and feet—but she was present, and she smiled as she opened her gifts. She was surrounded by love. And even in the darkest moments, Lizzie never lost her sense of humor. I remember one visit when the nurses were encouraging her to walk using a zimmer frame, trying to get her to the chair on the other side of the bed. Instead, she rolled over the bed and plopped down into the chair with a grin. She thought it was hilarious.

After weeks of intense physio, speech therapy, and support, Lizzie learned to eat again. Then to talk. Then walk. Then use the toilet. Inch by inch, she fought her way back. Finally, on July 31st, Lizzie was allowed to come home to continue her recovery. All MRIs done in hospital showed no sign of B-nard.

We had won the first battle.

Chapter 8- recovery begins at home

(told through the updates I posted on her page)

Facebook Post – 13th August 2021

I know some of you have been waiting for
an update. I've kept quiet so she's not
overwhelmed, but Lizzie is HOME!!!!
They decided that because she was doing so well, she
didn't need the stress of going to another hospital for
rehab. Instead, the rehab team would come to us. So now
we have regular visits from physio, a physio support
worker, occupational therapist, and SALT (Speech and
Language Therapy). It's very full on and Lizzie is
obviously exhausted—as am I, now being her carer. But
it's definitely better than her being away from us.
On the 19th August we were due to find out if she
would need radiotherapy. Thank you to everyone for

your love and support so far.

Ok, long post alert.

The good news: they cannot see any tumor on the newest MRI. However, due to the tumor's location, they couldn't leave a clear margin around it. That means even if it's not visible, it's likely some tumor cells remain. Because Lizzie's tumor is a stage 2 atypical meningioma, it's very likely to come back within five years if not completely destroyed. So, she will need radiotherapy. There are two options: standard radiotherapy—30 sessions, Monday to Friday—or proton beam therapy. Proton beam therapy is preferred because future side effects are less likely and less severe.

But it's only available in Manchester, which means Lizzie and I would have to live there for six weeks while it's done. Right now, Lizzie doesn't want to do that—she doesn't want to leave home.

There's also a risk of infertility with radiotherapy, so we've been referred to a fertility specialist to consider harvesting her eggs. Nothing is happening just yet, though, as she is still recovering. She will have another MRI in two months, then we'll meet with her consultant again to make a final decision. Most likely, treatment won't start until the new year. **25th September 2021**

Our whole family—me, Jason, Ellie, Kian, and Lizzie—took part in the Walk of Hope for Brain Tumor Research. Lizzie couldn't walk far yet, so she was in a wheelchair. But we did it—and raised £200.

Facebook Post – 3rd November 2021

Today we had a follow-up with Lizzie's surgeon, Mr. Chakraborty. To say he was happy with her progress is an understatement. He said she made his day.

We have a busy couple of weeks ahead. Tomorrow she has an MRI in Southampton. Then Friday, an ophthalmology appointment for her eyes. Next week she has an ultrasound in Lymington and then back to Southampton to see her radiologist, Dr. Clarke, to hopefully get the ball rolling with her proton beam therapy.

Facebook Post – 6th November 2021

Update from the optometrist: although her left eye still pulls all the way out and she sees double with both eyes open (damage caused by the tumor), her eyes are actually in pretty good shape. They've fogged up the lens on her left side so it's less obvious she has a patch. We go back in four months to check progress. They're hopeful it may correct itself. If not, she may need prism glasses—or, in the worst case, surgery.

Facebook Post – 18th January 2022

It's been a while, so quick update: Lizzie is doing well. She's still scared to walk outside, so we're working on building her confidence. Her eyes are still an issue, so surgery may be needed. We have an appointment with her radiologist on 17th February. Hopefully we'll get an MRI appointment soon and a clearer timeline for proton beam therapy.

Facebook Post – Early February 2022

Hi all—Lizzie is a bit upset right now. We were supposed to see her radiologist on the 17th to make a final decision about proton beam therapy. But because she hadn't been given an MRI appointment, it's now been pushed back to March 15th. She does have an MRI booked for 19th February, but the extra wait for results is causing her a lot of anxiety. She's very worried the tumor is growing back. Last night was tough.

We're seeing her CPN this morning, so hopefully that

will help support her mental health.

Facebook Post – 15th March 2022

The best possible news: no sign of the tumor! No need for radiotherapy either. Just regular MRIs now. If everything stays well, she'll have another in four months, then every six months for two years, then yearly for ten years. We can now start moving forward again.

Chapter 9 moving on

On the 7th of November 2022, Lizzie underwent surgery on her eye. It had been over a year since the tumor was removed, and despite all efforts, her vision hadn't improved on its own. Although she was walking again by now, her left side remained noticeably weaker, and she

lived with ongoing nerve pain. That hasn't gone away, even now. She relies on a walking stick to help her stay steady. It's just one of the many reminders of what she's endured. Thankfully, the eye surgery was a success. With a prism fitted into her glasses, her double vision was corrected, and for the first time in a long while, she could see clearly again. A small win, maybe, but for us, it felt enormous.

In January 2023, I began fundraising again for brain tumor research—something that had become very personal to us. It was during this time that I was contacted by BBC South Today. They had heard about Lizzie's journey and wanted to share her story. We were going to be on the news.

The interview went well. Lizzie was composed and thoughtful, speaking honestly about her experience, the trauma, the recovery, and her hopes for the future. The segment aired the following week. It was emotional watching it back, but so many people reached out—offering support, sharing their own stories, or simply saying how inspired they were by Lizzie's strength.

By 2024, Lizzie had made a life-changing decision: she wanted to return to education. Despite everything she had been through, or maybe because of it, she wanted to study psychology and sociology. She enrolled in an access course at college, determined to pursue something meaningful. I remember how proud we all were—especially knowing how difficult it had been for her to even leave the house again after everything. Now, in 2025, she's nearly finished the course. In September, she'll be starting university to study history—her true passion. A degree she once thought was beyond reach is now just beginning. Her resilience continues to astound me.

And the best part? Every single MRI since surgery has been clear.

Epilogue

It's hard to put into words how far we've come.

From that first terrifying MRI to sitting here now—watching Lizzie prepare for university, hearing her laugh, seeing her live—it all feels like a different lifetime. And yet, the memories are vivid. The fear, the hope, the strength we never knew we had—it's all still there, etched into us.

Lizzie's journey hasn't been easy. She faced the unimaginable and did it with grace, humour, and a quiet determination that continues to inspire everyone around her. There were days we didn't know what the future would hold. Days we didn't dare to hope. But she held on. We all did.

Today, Lizzie walks a little slower. Her body still carries the marks of what she's been through. But her mind—sharp, curious, strong—is ready to take on the world. And her heart? Bigger than ever.

This book is for the parents sitting in sterile hospital corridors, desperate for answers. For the young adults whose lives are thrown off course by something they never saw coming. For the carers, the siblings, the friends, the doctors, the nurses—and the warriors like Lizzie who remind us that even in our darkest moments, there is light. Through her eyes, we've seen pain, resilience, and unimaginable strength. Through mine, you've seen what it means to love, to fight, and to never give up hope.

This is not the end of the story. It's just a new chapter.

And B-nard? He's gone. Evicted. And he's not living rent-free in any of our heads ever again.

Photo Captions

MRI day — May 24, 2021The moment everything changed.

Admission dayLizzie arriving at the hospital after her MRI confirmed the presence of a brain tumor.

Post-biopsy recoveryLizzie smiling through pain, a few days after her brain biopsy. High-dependency unit — first surgeryPeaceful but critical hours following her first major brain operation.

Lizzie smiling after she tricked the nurses rolling over her bed   Even in the hardest moments, she found ways to laugh.

First trip out after coming homeA special moment outdoors, wrapped in love and pink warmth.

Fundraising day — Walk for HopeLizzie sharing joy and strength, giving back to those who helped her.

After her eye surgeryResting with her faithful plushies after a difficult but hopeful procedure. Lizzie now — joyful, creative, and unapologetically herself.

A survivor's light shines through.

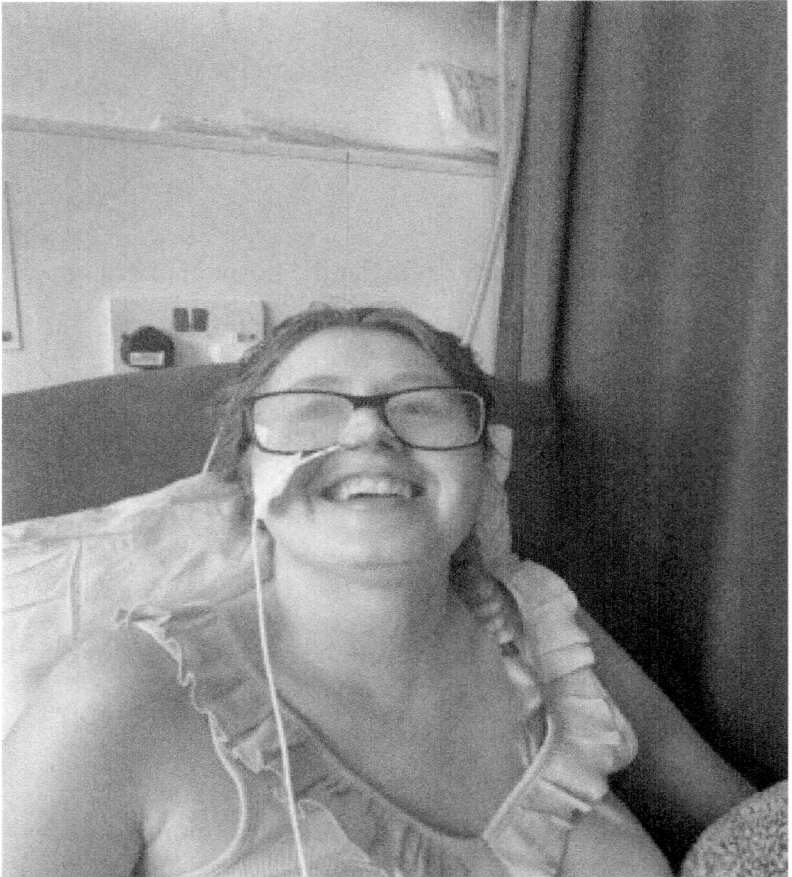

Lizzie smiling after
tricking the nurses,
rolling over the bed.

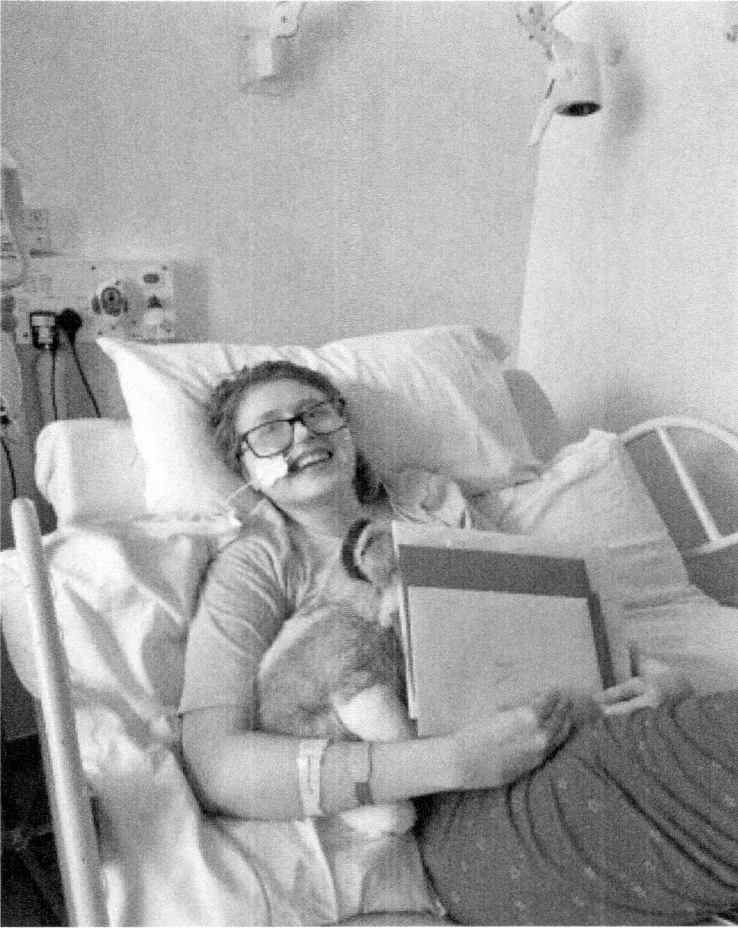
Lizzie celebrating her birthday in hospital, surrounded by cards, cuddles, and that ever-present smile.

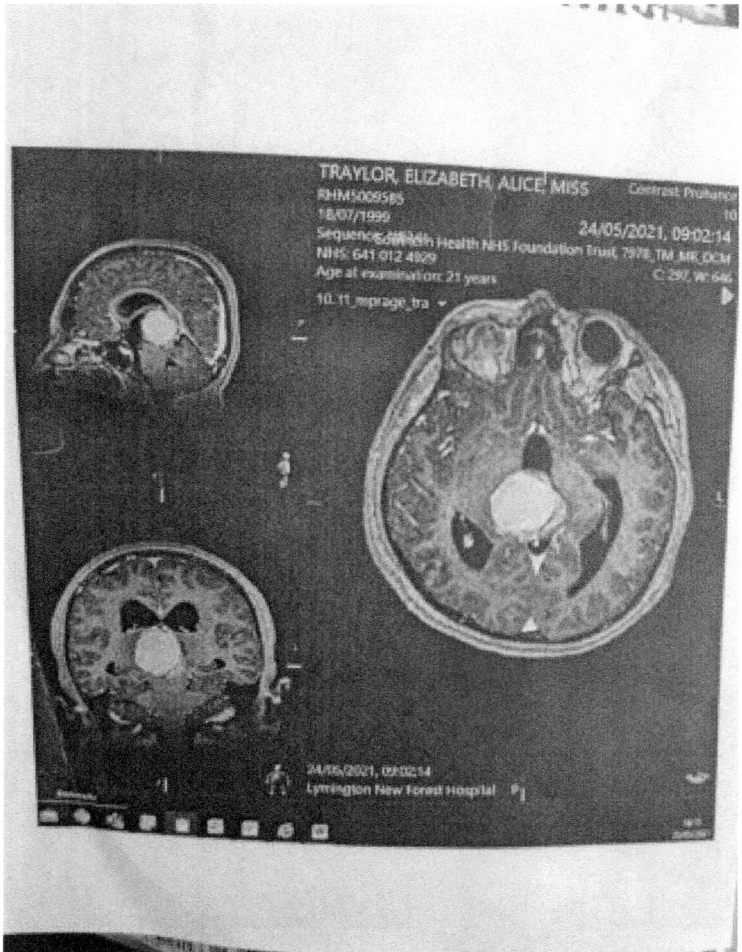

MRI scan taken on 24th May 2021 at Lymington New Forest Hospital, revealing the large brain tumor that marked the beginning of our journey.

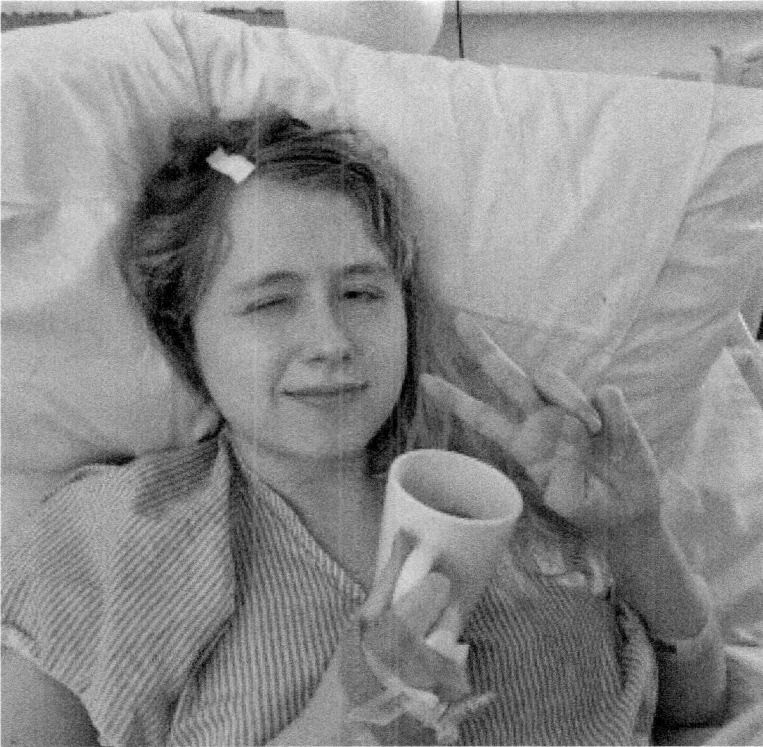
Lizzie after her brain biopsy—still smiling, still strong,
cup of tea in hand and peace sign up.

Fundraising day –
Walk for Hope, full of
love and strength.

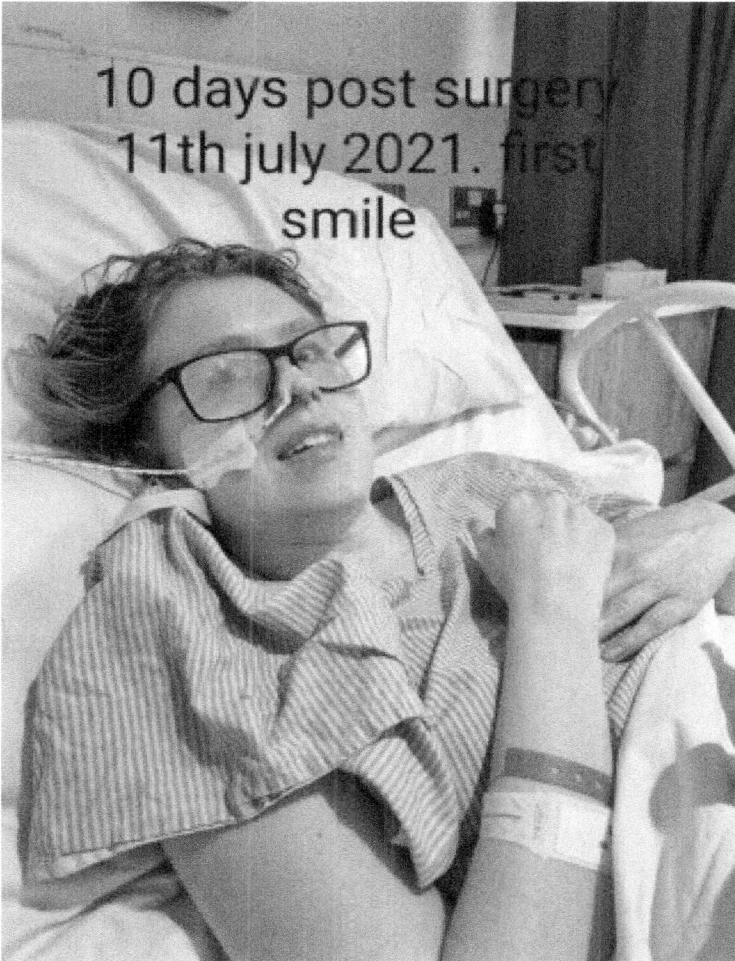

10 days
post-op –
11th July
2021.
First
smile.

First trip out after coming home –
wrapped in her pink blanket and
love.

Lizzie now — joyful,
creative, and
unapologetically
herself.

Printed in Dunstable, United Kingdom

63428518R00031